Biographies of th… …ge 2

CW01583783

EXTRAORDINARY ORDINARY PEOPLE

Clare Richards

Illustrated by Donald Melvin

Kevin Mayhew

First published in 2001 by
KEVIN MAYHEW LTD
Buxhall, Stowmarket, Suffolk IP14 3BW
E-mail: info@kevinmayhewltd.com

© 2001 Clare Richards and Donald Melvin

The right of Clare Richards and Donald Melvin to be identified as the authors of this work has been asserted by them in accordance with the Copyright, Designs and Patents Act 1988.

The contents of this book may be photocopied without copyright infringement, provided they are used for the purpose for which they are intended. Reproduction of any of the contents of this book for commercial purposes is subject to the usual copyright restrictions.

9 8 7 6 5 4 3 2 1 0

ISBN 1 84003 855 1
Catalogue No 1500485

Cover design by Angela Selfe
Edited and typeset by Elisabeth Bates

Contents

Reflections

Introduction

Christians are people who learn about God by following the example and teaching of his Son, Jesus. Jesus lived two thousand years ago. A man called Paul was the first to write about him and about the first Christians. Paul wrote letters to groups of Christians and he addressed them as *saints*. The word means 'holy' or 'sacred' and that really means 'god-like'. Paul expected Jesus' followers to be good people who became more like Jesus every day.

Today the word *saint* is more usually used to describe individual Christians who died as *heroes* of the Christian faith. Some great men, women and children lived extraordinary lives of love and care for others. Some were even killed because they believed that Jesus was God's Son and would not agree to stop following his teaching. We call these Christians *martyrs*. Some of the heroic Christians we read about in this book were *monks* and *nuns*. These are Christians who chose not to marry because they wanted to give all their time to serving the community and to prayer.

You will probably already have heard of several heroic Christians. In some towns even streets are named after them. In my city, we have St Stephen's Street, St Benedict's, St Augustine's and St Giles' Street. Of course churches are often named after a saint. Have you heard of the great St Paul's Cathedral in London? Some of the heroic Christians of the past have been chosen by groups or by countries to be their representatives: they are given the name *patron saints*. St George is the patron saint of England.

Christians have always made journeys or *pilgrimages* to holy places. Many have travelled to the Holy Land where Jesus lived and died. Many more have gone on pilgrimage to the places associated with the saints. When famous and heroic Christians died, the people who knew and admired them often built decorated tombs to hold their bones (*relics*). These burial places were respected as holy places and were often visited by Christians. They are known as *shrines*, and are usually found in great churches or cathedrals. Pilgrims go to Rome to visit the shrine of St Peter or to Canterbury to the shrine of Archbishop Thomas Becket.

Two groups or denominations, Roman Catholics and Orthodox, select outstanding Christians of the past and officially call them Saints. But we shouldn't forget that Paul expected all followers of Jesus to deserve the title – with a small 's'.

Thomas Aquinas b. 1225

Holy Day: 28 January

Many years ago there lived a little boy who asked everyone he met the same question: 'What is God like?' He never stopped asking that question all his life. The boy was Thomas who came from a rich Italian family. Thomas went to school at Monte Cassino, where he was taught by Benedictine monks. They helped him find some answers to his questions about God. He was far more interested in that than in football! (He was never athletic; later he got so fat they had to cut his shape into the table so he could reach his food.)

Thomas was very clever and everyone expected him to go to university and become a wealthy professor. But Thomas had learnt that money wasn't everything and that prayer was important too. So while at university he shocked his family and friends by joining a group of poor men who called themselves 'brothers' or friars, begging for food and preaching about God. His family thought this was rather a waste of his talents. So they kidnapped Thomas and kept him shut away for a whole year. He did not change his mind. He became a friar and continued his studies in Paris and then in Cologne. His companions were called Friars Preachers, or 'Blackfriars', because they wore black robes. Today we usually call them Dominicans after their founder, St Dominic.

Dominic died when Thomas was a young boy. Thomas had probably heard that he was a remarkable preacher. Dominic had travelled all across Europe explaining the Gospel. This had begun when the Pope asked him to go to France to preach because some people there were getting very twisted ideas about God. Pope Innocent III wanted Dominic to put them right. When others joined him they formed a new Order of scholars who studied and preached about God. (We call them theologians.) Dominic was a great leader. He cared very much about people, especially the poor and those who suffered. He chose to live like the poor. So it is not surprising that Thomas decided to join these followers of Dominic.

Thomas became a great teacher himself, but he is best known for his writings. His two great works, called the *Summa Theologica* and the *Summa Contra Gentiles*, are still important to theologians today. In these volumes Thomas kept exploring his favourite question: 'What is God like?' He said it is easier to know what God is *not* like, but he believed we can get close to God by faith, study and prayer. That is exactly what he did.

Think about it

Never stop asking important questions.

SAINT THOMAS AQUINAS
SAINT DOMINIC

John Bosco b. 1815

Holy Day: 31 January

John Bosco's father died when he was only 2. His mother, now a single parent, worked hard on their small farm in Italy to make ends meet. He and his brothers grew up to be a great help to her. When he was 9 he had a dream that was to influence the rest of his life. He saw wild beasts turning into gentle lambs and disobedient children becoming well behaved. He was convinced that he ought to become a priest so that he could help people. So that is what he did.

John had been born into a troubled Europe. The early nineteenth century was a time of war, and the beginning of the Industrial Revolution. Many people moved to the towns looking for work, and it caused great poverty and restlessness. John discovered that many young boys were getting into trouble. Some had nowhere to go when thrown out of prison. So as a well-trained young priest, he set up a home for boys called the Oratory of St Francis de Sales. He chose this saint as his patron because he admired his spirit of gentleness. It was said that through all the many years John Bosco worked with difficult boys, he never punished them or acted fiercely. He won them over with patience and kindness.

Other priests joined John to help in the work, and he called his helpers Salesians (after St Francis de Sales). With the help of a peasant woman, Mary Mazzarello, he also founded a congregation to help girls. Both organisations developed so quickly, that in a few years there were hundreds of priests and nuns caring for young people in hostels, schools, workshops and training centres. Their work spread across Europe.

It was said that John Bosco had remarkable influence on the young people of his day. He found a way to make religion and school work attractive by allowing plenty of time for sport and recreation. He was always over-busy, running his schools and communities, raising funds, sorting out awkward town and Church officials, and attending to the needs of the poor. Yet he was never known to be impatient, or to turn away from someone in need. Just before he died, suffering from eczema and failing eyesight, he travelled across France and Spain on a fund-raising trip. He had enormous trust in God, and when things were difficult, always said, 'God will help us'.

Think about it
God helps those who help themselves.

SAINT
JOHN
BOSCO

BRIGID — FIFTH CENTURY

HOLY DAY: 1 FEBRUARY

St Brigid is dearly loved in Ireland, and even in countries as far away as Australia and New Zealand. This is not surprising because she was a charming and compassionate woman. Everyone who met her must have loved her. Brigid had an unusual background. Her father was a pagan chieftain called Dubthach, and her mother Brocessa was a Christian slave. They lived near Dundalk in Ireland in the fifth century.

It was not easy for Brocessa to bring up her daughter as a Christian, but she certainly succeeded. Brigid was a happy and generous girl and often got into trouble with her father for giving away food to the poor. She even gave away his sword. No one was surprised when Brigid became a nun. In those days nuns continued to live at home, following a rule of prayer and helping the local church. Brigid changed that. She thought they could serve people better by living in groups. She quickly set up religious communities throughout the land. The largest and best known was at Kildare, a double monastery for monks and nuns.

Many legends grew up about Brigid, and it is difficult to tell which of these stories are true. Strange tales were told of her adventures as she travelled across Ireland. Yet it is clear from all the stories that she was energetic, loved music and laughter, and above all was the most generous-hearted woman you could ever meet. She gave away everything. One friend brought her a box of apples, and watched her hand them out to the poor who were always at her gate. She didn't keep one for herself. Her community complained that when people gave them treasures, Brigid sold them to buy food for those worse off than themselves.

Brigid loved to work on the convent farm. She looked after the sheep, helped with the harvest, made the butter and was well known for her home-brewed ale. Like many of the Celtic saints, she had a real love for animals and wildlife; she is said to have tamed foxes and wild boar. Ducks followed her everywhere. Brigid lived an uncomplicated life of ordinary hard work and prayer, yet the Church in Ireland recognised her greatness even in her lifetime. She lived to be 70, and was buried at Kildare. Later her body was taken to Downpatrick, to be buried alongside St Patrick himself.

THINK ABOUT IT

Would you give away your last Rolo, or even the whole packet?

SAINT BRIGID

VALENTINE — THIRD CENTURY

HOLY DAY: 14 FEBRUARY

How many of you had a Valentine's Day card last February? We all look forward to receiving one. The strange thing is that we know almost nothing about St Valentine, except that he was a Roman saint in the early Church.

All that Church historians can discover is that a church was built in the fourth century on the Flaminian Way, the main road north out of Rome. It was in honour of a priest called Valentine, who was beheaded there about the year 269. This was during the persecutions under the Roman emperor known as Claudius the Goth. But the story is complicated because a second martyr called Valentine is commemorated on the same day. This beheaded martyr was a bishop, and was put to death in a different district of Rome. There could have been two saints, but it is more likely that one person called Valentine was martyred, and two traditions grew up about him.

There is nothing in the legend of this saint to connect him with the custom of sending cards and choosing partners on 14 February. It is perhaps linked to the old idea that birds always began to pair on this date. But one thing we do know about some birds is that when they mate they stay faithful to their partner. This is a good symbol and example for couples who love each other. It may not be so strange to have a saint as patron of loving couples, because love is at the heart of Jesus' teaching.

Sending a card to someone means you are telling them, 'You are special'. Jesus pointed out that everyone is special. In fact, he said that people are so special to God that he will always provide for them. Jesus said, 'Look at the birds: they don't sow seeds, gather a harvest and put it in barns; yet your Father in heaven takes care of them! Aren't you worth much more than birds?' When you really love someone you will take care of them.

The pair of love-birds that may be the source of St Valentine's Day is an appropriate symbol for Christians who believe that love, faithfulness and care for one another is how we are meant to live if we are to be God's children.

THINK ABOUT IT

When you love someone you take care of them.

SAINT:
VALENTINE:

DAVID

BORN ABOUT 460

HOLY DAY: 1 MARCH

What do you think might be the connection between David the king of the Jews, and David the patron saint of Wales? It must be music. It is believed that King David played the harp, and wrote some of the psalms ('poems' about God) that are still sung in churches and cathedrals. St David would have sung those psalms. Being Welsh he probably sang them very well because the Welsh have good singing voices.

David (Dewi in Welsh) was born in Cardigan, Wales, in the fifth century. His father, Sant, was a local chieftain and his mother, Non, was a very good mother. She was later called a saint and churches were named after her. Influenced by his good parents, David became a monk and later a bishop. He too must have lived a holy life because so many places, churches and monasteries were named after him.

In those early days of Christianity, the Celtic monks travelled around the country setting up small communities. David set up his first monastery in Menevia on the north-Pembrokeshire coast. He eventually set up more than fifty churches where prayer was led by the monks. The life they lived was very hard. They worked in the fields and kept absolute silence, not even speaking to each other. They ate only enough food to survive and often fasted. David was known as the 'Waterman' because he wouldn't let his monks drink anything but water.

David was present at an important meeting (Synod) at Brefi in Cardiganshire. He influenced the decisions that were made about the way monks should live. In the Middle Ages many stories were told about David. They may not be true, but showed how much people thought of him. There was a story that while he was speaking at Brefi, the field he stood in was raised up into a hill, and a dove flew onto his shoulder. It probably means that he was a man of peace.

The people also wanted to show how important the Church was in Wales, so they said that Bishop David had gone to Jerusalem (the city of King David) to be made an archbishop. We don't know this, but we know his last words; they were, 'Be cheerful, keep the faith.' So he was probably a very cheerful person himself.

THINK ABOUT IT
Be cheerful and you will make others happy.

SAINT · DAVID · 46º A · D ·

JOHN WESLEY — B. 1703

HOLY DAY: 2 MARCH

Can you imagine a crowd of 20,000 people? If you've been to a crowded football match at Norwich City, Burnley or Millwall, you'll have some idea. A pop concert will get this sort of crowd too. A preacher called John Wesley drew crowds of 20,000 people when he spoke about Jesus. That was 250 years ago.

John's father was the Anglican rector of Epworth in Lincolnshire, in the early eighteenth century. The family were happy, and it was not surprising that John and his younger brother Charles chose to go to Oxford University to study for the priesthood. As a young priest in the Church of England, John even helped in his father's parish. At university Charles and his friends were so enthusiastic about following their religious practices that they became known as the 'Holy Club' or the 'Oxford Methodists'. When John returned to Oxford as a teacher he joined the group.

John and Charles were so enthusiastic about following Jesus that they decided to be missionaries and went out to Georgia in America. They were over-eager; it only annoyed people, so they returned home. But John never lost his enthusiasm and began to preach to his congregations in England with extraordinary zeal. Most parish clergy were living rather comfortable lives and worried about an enthusiastic audience, so they refused to let him preach in their churches. This didn't stop John. He got on his horse and rode into country villages, preaching in the open air. He took the Gospel out to people, rather as Jesus had done. John set up his first small church (chapel) in Bristol. He was joined there by Charles, and they adopted the name 'Methodist'. The two brothers had moved away from the Church of England and were becoming more evangelical. John wanted to be more active and involved in preaching the Gospel with enthusiasm. He wanted to influence the lives of ordinary people. For 50 years he travelled across England, addressing huge gatherings of farmers, miners, weavers and casual town workers. The people loved him and he set up many Methodist chapels across the country.

John could not be everywhere at once, so he wrote sermons and books. Both brothers wrote hymns. They were so popular that he earned thousands of pounds. He gave it all away to help the poor. When he died in 1791, his followers split away from the Church of England. They used his writings as the guidelines to set up the Methodist Church. John had not wanted to leave the Church of England; he would have been rather sad.

THINK ABOUT IT
When one door closes – open another one.

CHARLESTON
ATLANTA
SAVANNAH
NEW ORLEANS
JACKSONVILLE
ORLANDO
MIAMI
JOHN WESLEY B. 1703 • D. 1791

FRANCES OF ROME — B. 1384

HOLY DAY: 9 MARCH

Most of the saints officially recognised by the Church are priests, nuns, bishops or kings. But we all know that some of the best people in the world are mums and dads, who just get on with bringing up families without any fuss. Frances of Rome could be nominated as patron saint of mothers. She was born into a rich and important Roman family at a time when life was really hard. There was a civil war in Italy, and constant epidemics of the killer plague.

Frances married Lorenzo de' Ponziani when she was only 13. The young couple had several children, but two died very young. Perhaps it was this sadness that made the young mother very concerned for other families who suffered. She was known for her kindness and her prayerful life. She was working hard at running the household and caring for the children, when disaster struck. Their home was destroyed by an army from Naples, and her husband had to go into hiding while she continued to keep the family together. Lorenzo returned five years later, but he was a broken man. Frances had to care for him for over twenty years. When he died in 1436, they had been married for forty years. It is said that they never had an argument in all that time!

Frances was such a good example to her neighbours in Rome that some other ladies joined her in helping the poor and sick. She organised them into a society, and asked the Benedictine monks of Monte Oliveto to help them. They bought a house as their work centre, and those who lived there as a small community were called Oblates of Tor de' Specchi. Frances joined the group herself when all her children had grown up. It is an amazing fact that 550 years later there is still a community in Rome continuing their work.

Many stories were told about Frances which describe her prayerful and charitable life. Some are so strange that they read like legends. She has even been made patron saint of motorists, who go in thousands to her church in Rome on her Holy Day. She clearly made an enormous impression on her family and friends, and she became a highly respected and loved person; no one respected her more than the Pope, Eugenius IV. Her family home is still a place of pilgrimage.

THINK ABOUT IT
Parents are precious – treasure them.

SAINT
FRANCES
OF ROME

PATRICK B. 385?

HOLY DAY: 17 MARCH

What is your favourite colour? If you are Irish the chances are that you will like green. Ireland's international football and rugby teams turn out in green shirts; the land is known as the Emerald Isle and the country's symbol is the green shamrock. On 17 March, Dublin's O'Connell Street and New York's Fifth Avenue are a sea of green flags as crowds celebrate in carnival style. Even the beer is coloured green!

The celebrations are in honour of St Patrick, the fifth-century saint who is said to have converted the Irish to Christianity. Before he died Patrick wrote briefly about his own life. So we know that his father, a Roman tax collector, was called Calpurnius and was a member of the council ruling a settlement somewhere along the coast of Wales. He had a comfortable childhood but his happiness was shattered when he was 16 years old. Pirates raided his settlement and took Patrick, and many others, across the sea to Ireland. He was sold as a slave. He was made to wear a sheepskin tunic and sandals and his head was shaved. For six long years he worked as a herdsman of swine on a lonely hillside, probably in Antrim.

It was during this silent time, amongst the green hills, that Patrick thought about God and learned to pray. After six years he plotted an escape and managed to get back home. But he left his family again to study and become a priest. He once had a vivid dream that he should return to Ireland. And he did – as a missionary bishop. There were already some Christians in Ireland but it was Patrick who travelled far and wide, preaching the Gospel and teaching the people to love God.

Patrick was such a good preacher that churches and monasteries were soon built across the land. But he had many difficulties to overcome. He met fierce opposition from some leaders and was even accused by other priests of being too ambitious. He always thought he was not very clever and he knew that many people disliked him. It made him depressed and sad, especially when his best friend suddenly turned against him – just when he needed his support. Patrick often longed to return home to Britain, but he never did, believing that God wanted him to stay in his adopted country. He could never have imagined that he would be remembered and loved, century after century, across the world.

THINK ABOUT IT

A friend can let you down, but God never will.

SAINT
PATRICK

JOSEPH — FIRST CENTURY

HOLY DAY: 19 MARCH

St Joseph is the quiet saint. We don't know very much about him – and yet he is remembered on two days, so he must be very important. Indeed he is, because he chose Mary, the mother of Jesus, to be his wife. He was a father to Jesus, teaching him by his example and words to become the compassionate, honest, loving person we read about in the Gospels.

From the Gospels we learn that Joseph was a descendant of King David. But this royal descent did not make him rich and important. The story Luke tells suggests he was rather poor. His family belonged to Bethlehem, David's city, but he had moved to Nazareth in the north. He was a carpenter and builder and may have found some work mending the boats of fishermen who lived by the Sea of Galilee. He was probably a young man when he met Mary and proposed to her. A later tradition imagined he was quite old and widowed. This was because Joseph disappears from the Gospel story about Jesus, and does not appear at Mary's side when Jesus was preaching. So he must have died before Jesus was crucified.

We have no recorded words that Joseph spoke, but Matthew and Luke left a sharp outline of his character. He was a patient, reliable man who was full of unquestioning faith in God's ways. He quietly observed the Jewish Law, accepted hardships, faithfully protected his family and worked hard to provide for them. There seems a calm dignity about him which the Church has recognised by proclaiming him the perfect model for ordinary working people.

Some Christians call him 'Joseph the worker' and remember him on International Labour Day, 1 May. He is a good example of a hard-working labourer. It reminds us that, while some jobs carry greater responsibility, no job is more important than any other. Joseph was a simple craftsman who used his hands to build and mend broken furniture or leaking boats. Builders, school cleaners and shop assistants are just as important as doctors, politicians, scientists and headteachers. Jesus learned this lesson from St Joseph and probably worked alongside him for most of his life. They learned together that the greatest happiness comes from doing a job well, because in that way we show that we love our neighbour as much as we love ourselves.

THINK ABOUT IT

A school dinner lady is as important as the head-teacher.

SAINT JOSEPH

Cuthbert b. 634

Holy Day: 20 March

When Cuthbert was a young boy he looked after his father's sheep on the hillside above Leader Water in Scotland. The story is told that when he was 16 he had a vision of Bishop Aidan of Lindisfarne being taken to heaven by angels. He was certainly influenced by the life of this holy monk, because he left home to join a monastery at Melrose.

As a young monk, he travelled hundreds of miles on horseback and on foot to keep Christianity alive amongst scattered communities in southern Scotland. In 664 he and his friend Eata went to Lindisfarne in Northumbria. Eata became the abbot of the community and later its bishop, and Cuthbert was elected as prior of the monastery. Everyone quickly recognised Cuthbert's extraordinary gift for understanding people. He was a wonderful listener, and shared all the joys and sorrows of those who came to him for guidance. In a remarkable way he was able to reconcile people who had been divided by their race or their ideals.

Prior Cuthbert loved the whole of creation and became the protector of the sea-birds that lived on his island. He often wandered around Lindisfarne during the summer evenings to admire the beauty of nature, and quietly praise God. He even became an amateur archaeologist. It is remarkable that after a few years Cuthbert chose to live completely alone on the deserted Isle of Farne, across the water from his community. He loved to be with people, yet he chose to live as a hermit. Eight years later the local Church begged Cuthbert to become the bishop of Hexham. He accepted reluctantly, but immediately exchanged places with his friend Bishop Eata of Lindisfarne. So he returned to his monastery to become a generous leader who gave all his time to others. And as bishop he travelled around his diocese with wholehearted zeal, especially helping those in trouble.

Bishop Cuthbert was loved so much that many stories arose about the wonderful things he did. The people of Northumbria were heartbroken when his energy failed and he returned to his lonely Isle of Farne to prepare for death. When he died the news was signalled to Lindisfarne by the waving of torches from the cliff top. He was buried at Lindisfarne but later was moved to a shrine in Durham Cathedral.

Think about it

The whole of creation praises God just by being there.

SAINT : CUTHBERT

GEORGE

George — Third or Fourth Century

Holy Day: 23 April

In the parkland surrounding the United Nations building in New York there are several statues and pieces of sculpture. The most outstanding is a larger-than-life model of St George on his horse killing the dragon. It was a gift from Russia in 1990. St George is greatly honoured in the Russian Orthodox Church and is the patron saint of England. Strangely very little is known about George, even though he became the most famous of the early Christian martyrs.

St George's life contains a number of legends. These are stories that grew up about him but cannot be proved to have really happened. Nevertheless these legends tell us that people believed in his goodness and in his courage. It does seem likely that George was martyred in Lydda, Palestine, at the close of the third century. Many Christians were killed at that time for refusing to give up their belief in Jesus. George was admired as a soldier-saint from these early times. In the Middle Ages, when knights were admired for defending their cities, St George became very popular as the model knight. One book called the *Golden Legend* described him as a knight from Cappadocia who rescued a young lady from a dragon. It was said to have taken place in Libya and led to thousands of baptisms.

St George was made the patron saint of England, probably when King Edward III founded the Order of the Garter under his protection. This was in 1348. The Queen awards special people the title of the Order of the Garter at a ceremony in St George's Chapel, Windsor. He is patron saint of soldiers and of the Scout and Guide Movement. The badge of St George, a red cross on a white background, was already seen in the Middle Ages in Western art. In the East, icons (sacred paintings) frequently show St George wearing a red cloak over armour, riding on a white horse.

In the story of St George and the dragon, the people of the town could only reach their water supply by giving the dragon a human sacrifice. St George killed the dragon, rescued the king's daughter and made it possible for the people to have freedom and the water they needed to live. The sculpture at the United Nations in New York uses this legend and teaches us an important lesson: St George is killing a dragon whose body is made up of actual nuclear missiles. It is called *Good Defeats Evil*.

Think about it
It takes courage for goodness to overcome badness.

The Legend of St. George and the Dragon

St. George travelled for many months by land and sea until he came to Libya. Here he met a poor hermit who told him that everyone in that land was in great distress, for a dragon had long ravaged the country.

'Every day,' said the old man, 'he demands the sacrifice of a beautiful maiden and now all the young girls have been killed. The king's daughter alone remains, and unless we can find a knight who can slay the dragon she will be sacrificed tomorrow. The king of Egypt will give his daughter in marriage to the champion who overcomes this terrible monster.'

When St. George heard this story, he was determined to try and save the princess, so he rested that night in the hermit's hut, and at daybreak set out to the valley where the dragon lived. When he drew near he saw a little procession of women, headed by a beautiful girl dressed in pure Arabian silk. The princess Sabra was being led by her attendants to the place of death. The knight spurred his horse and overtook the ladies. He comforted them with brave words and persuaded the princess to return to the palace. Then he entered the valley.

As soon as the dragon saw him it rushed from its cave, roaring with a sound louder than thunder. Its head was immense and its tail fifty feet long. But St. George was not afraid. He struck the monster with his spear, hoping he would wound it.

The dragon's scales were so hard that the spear broke into a thousand pieces. and St. George fell from his horse. Fortunately he rolled under an enchanted orange tree against which poison could not prevail, so that the venomous dragon was unable to hurt him. Within a few minutes he had recovered his strength and was able to fight again.

He smote the beast with his sword, but the dragon poured poison on him and his armour split in two. Once more he refreshed himself from the orange tree and then, with his sword in his hand, he rushed at the dragon and pierced it under the wing where there were no scales, so that it fell dead at his feet.

SAINT GEORGE

Catherine of Siena b. 1347

Holy Day: 29 April

Siena is a fine city in Italy. It was there that Catherine was born in 1347, the youngest of a very large family. They lived in a comfortable house where their father Giacomo Benincasa was a successful wool-dyer. Catherine was the noisiest of the children. When she became a teenager she surprised everyone by spending hours quietly in her room, happy to read and pray. Her mother was unhappy because Catherine refused to wear fine dresses and didn't want to go to parties. The family called her 'the difficult teenager'.

They couldn't understand Catherine when she turned down marriage and just as definitely refused to become a nun. She was a very strong-willed young lady. Eventually she chose to belong to the Third Order of St Dominic. This meant she could wear the black and white dress of Dominican nuns and follow part of their Rule, but remain at home. Catherine spent hours praying and thinking about the life of Jesus. Sometimes she was not even aware of anyone near her when she was praying. (We call this 'mystical' prayer.) After years spent quietly at home, Catherine went out to nurse the sick and care for the poor.

Most people of Siena recognised that they had an extraordinary person in their midst. She was full of laughter and deeply prayerful at the same time. Above all she had a remarkable ability to give helpful advice to people. A group gathered round her – priests, noblemen, rich ladies, soldiers, artists, the poor and uneducated, both young and old. They became known as her 'family' or the 'Caterinati', and they supported her in her future work.

At this time there was a crisis in the Church. The Pope had left Rome and was living in France, in Avignon. It was the cause of trouble between the two countries, and in 1375 Catherine was asked to intervene. She urged Pope Gregory to return to Rome, but every opposition was put in his way, and she was treated badly. Eventually Catherine won the battle of wills, and the Pope returned to Rome. This was only the beginning of a new row. When Pope Gregory died, two Popes were elected – one in Rome and one in France. It was the beginning of a bad time for the Church. Catherine died in Rome when she was trying to solve the problem. Her parents would have been proud of their determined and holy daughter.

Think about it

If you keep knocking at a door, it will eventually open.

VIEW OF THE DUOMO

VIEW TOWARDS THE DUOMO - OLD PALACE

PALACE COURTYARD

SAINT
CATHERINE
OF SIENA

Bede the Venerable b. 673

Holy Day: 25 May

Have you ever been to the public library? If not, you will certainly have been into your school library. Did you know that the first libraries were set up by monks? One monk who spent hours in his library was called Bede. He was a Geordie, born south of the River Tyne at Jarrow. He went to a monastic school when he was 7, and stayed on to become a deacon at the age of 18. Later he became a priest.

You could hardly call Bede a great traveller: he scarcely ever left the twin monasteries of Wearmouth and Jarrow, and they were practically next door to his family home! His life was uneventful too; he quietly carried out the duties of his monastery, working and praying. He had no visions, worked no miracles and was not visited by kings or bishops. But Bede was to be remembered across Europe for his remarkable skill in teaching and writing. He spent hours in the library studying subjects in detail, then he shared his knowledge with his pupils and wrote down his notes. These were published and became, even in his lifetime, very important records. So they called him 'venerable' which means 'worthy of respect'.

Bede was especially interested in Scripture, science and history. He wrote commentaries on the Bible by comparing the thoughts of earlier Christian thinkers (called the 'Fathers'). He studied Greek and a little Hebrew so that he could understand the Bible better. His scientific writings were mostly about ways of calculating the calendar to make an accurate date for Easter; and he also recorded traditional explanations for natural events like storms and famines. But it is his historical writings that are best remembered today. He wrote a church history book that is the main source for the history of Saxon times. His works were carefully written and can be found on many library shelves even today.

Bede only left his monastery twice; once when he was sent to visit Archbishop Egbert's schools in York as a kind of 'OFSTED' inspector, and once to visit Lindisfarne. Everyone visited Lindisfarne, the great island monastery built by Aidan. Bede went there to do research for his book on the lives of the saints. He always looked for accurate sources and good witnesses. Bede suffered badly from asthma, but he worked until the last hour of his life. He dictated the final sentence of his book on St John and died.

Think about it
Even the most ordinary job is worth doing well.

SAINT BEDE THE VENERABLE

Joan of Arc b. 1412

Holy Day: 30 May

Joan's parents were peasant farmers, who owned enough land to grow their own food. They lived in the countryside of Champagne in France. Joan, the youngest of five children, loved to play in the village, around the 'fairy tree'. She never went to school but learnt from her mother how to cook and sew, and also how to pray. It was an ideal childhood, only spoilt by the constant fighting between England and France (where the whole of Burgundy had joined the English side).

When Joan was about 13 she had the first of some strange experiences; she heard voices telling her that she must save France from the English occupation. Joan being a sensible girl was reluctant to do anything. But eventually she saw the dauphin – the heir to the throne, and he believed her. He sent her to important churchmen who questioned her. She had a hard time convincing them, but in the end everyone believed her.

So Joan became a soldier. This was remarkable: a young girl, dressed as a boy in armour, and leading soldiers out to battle. Ten days later the French army defeated the English. But things did not go well for her. Although she persuaded the dauphin to be crowned king of France, he was a lazy, weak character. Joan insisted that the war was not over, and prepared for more battles. But King Charles was too slow to follow her advice. Joan went on her own into the war-zone and was captured. The king left her to her fate. She was sold to the English.

The English army could not condemn Joan for beating them in battle, so they had her tried in the religious court. There she was treated roughly. She was accused of being a witch and of making up her voices. Yet she stood up to her accusers quite fearlessly, and never doubted her conscience, her 'heavenly voices'. Joan was found guilty and handed over to the law. She was only 19 when she was burnt to death in the market-place of Rouen. King Charles never came to help her. Some years later the Pope re-examined the case and found that her accusers had acted dishonestly, for political reasons. Eventually the Church made Joan a saint, not for being a brave soldier, but because she was absolutely honest and followed her conscience, even when it meant death.

Think about it

Do you always listen to your conscience?

SAINT
JOAN
OF ARC

BONIFACE — B. 675

HOLY DAY: 5 JUNE

Boniface. Now that's an interesting name. Could it mean this saint was very good-looking, or that he had a fine complexion from eating all those Devonshire cream teas? No, in fact, he was actually christened Wynfrith, and grew up in the Devonshire town of Crediton, but he changed his name to Boniface in honour of a Roman martyr.

Wynfrith was sent to school at the Benedictine monastery in Exeter. Then he became a monk and was sent to a monastery at Nursling, near Southampton. He became a good teacher (he wrote the first Latin grammar book for English students), and was known far and wide for being an outstanding priest. He was very friendly and people loved him. In 717 Wynfrith was elected abbot of Nursling, but he said that he would rather become a missionary monk in Germany, in a region which in those days was called Frisia.

Wynfrith went to Rome to get the Pope's blessing, and that is when he changed his name to Boniface. From then on he became an enthusiastic missionary, travelling far and wide across western Germany, converting thousands to Christianity and setting up Benedictine monasteries. On a visit back to Rome, Boniface was made a bishop and he set up his home in Mainz. He never returned to England although he always kept writing to his English friends. Some of these, both monks and nuns, went to join him in Germany to help him in his work.

Pope Gregory III made Boniface an Archbishop, and invited him to organise all the Church dioceses in Germany, working alongside King Pepin the Short. Even when Boniface was over 70 he kept on working, this time in Holland. But, like his namesake the first Boniface, he died a martyr, killed by pagans while he was confirming some new Christians. The Archbishop of Canterbury wrote to the monks in Germany: 'We in England loved Boniface, and count him among the best and greatest teachers of the faith.' He was buried in the Benedictine monastery at Fulda. It is rather sad that, although Boniface is loved and honoured by German Christians, he is often forgotten in England.

THINK ABOUT IT
Would Boniface support England, Germany or Holland in the World Cup?

SAINT : BONIFACE :

ANTHONY OF PADUA — B. 1195

HOLY DAY: 13 JUNE

St Anthony is a curious saint. Almost everything he did in life seems to have been forgotten the moment he died. Stories grew up about him and he was said to have worked hundreds of miracles. Artists drew him, and statues were made that presented him as a gentle Franciscan carrying a lily in one hand and the Child Jesus on his arm. Anthony did become a Franciscan, but there is little evidence of the extraordinary happenings. Padua is in Italy, yet Anthony was not an Italian.

So who was he? In 1195 a baby was born into the family of a knight who served in the court of King Alfonso II of Portugal. The baby was called Ferdinand. He had a fine upbringing and was sent to the cathedral school in Lisbon. When he was only 15 Ferdinand became an Augustinian monk and moved to Coimbra, where he became an outstanding biblical and theological scholar. He was also guest-master in the community and one day looked after five Franciscan friars who were on their way to Morocco. Later he heard that they had been murdered. Immediately Ferdinand felt he should take their place. He left the Augustinians and became a Franciscan, taking the name Anthony. He went to Morocco to work among the Moslems, but had to return because of ill-health.

Anthony lived quietly in a community of Friars in Italy where no one really noticed him. One day a visiting preacher didn't turn up and Anthony was told at the last minute to preach the sermon. He astonished everyone by his words. He was immediately sent out to preach the Gospel across Italy. He did this for seven years. The crowds could not fit into the churches and platforms had to be built so that he could address thousands at a time. His words were strong and fearless; he attacked the rich for their selfishness and priests for their weakness. He once told a bishop off, shouting: 'You with the mitre on, I'm talking about you!'

Anthony died in Padua when he was only 36, and was buried in the cathedral. His shrine became a place of pilgrimage and the memory of this outspoken preacher was lost. It was replaced by the image of a gentle saint who cares about ordinary people's small problems. There must have been something very special about this saint that he is so admired and loved.

THINK ABOUT IT

Are you brave enough to speak out when things are wrong?

SAINT ANTHONY OF PADUA

ALBAN DIED IN THE THIRD CENTURY

HOLY DAY: 22 JUNE

During the lifetime of Jesus, Palestine was under Roman rule because it was part of the Roman Empire. Britain also became part of this empire. There are still many remains of great Roman towns across the country. You might live in or near one – York, Chester, London, or Winchester for example. Just north of Roman London there was a smaller town called Verulamium. Later it became an important city not because of the Romans, but because of a man called Alban.

Alban lived in Verulamium in the third century; we describe him as a Romano-Briton. At this time the Roman emperor Diocletian was afraid of the growing number of Christians, and began to persecute them, sending out his soldiers to get rid of them. Alban was not a Christian, but he was a good and fair man. He offered to hide a Christian priest in his home. When soldiers searched the house, Alban put on the priest's cloak and was taken away in his place. When the judge discovered this he was furious. He commanded Alban to offer sacrifice to the Roman gods, but Alban refused, saying he had become a Christian. He was taken away and killed. And from that moment he was honoured as a Christian martyr.

The story of Alban was described in more detail later, especially by St Bede in the seventh century (see page 32). He described how crowds followed Alban as he was led outside the city to the river. Alban prayed and the river dried up to let him through. At this his soldier-executioner threw away the sword and offered to die with him. The procession went up a flower-covered hill where the two men were executed. Bede said that it was a place worthy by its beauty to receive the blood of the martyrs. When Bede recorded the lives of early saints he used imaginative ways to show that God was with them, but his stories are believed to be based on firm historical facts.

The tomb of St Alban became a place of pilgrimage, and a church and shrine was built over it. In 793 the Anglo-Saxon king Offa built a great Benedictine monastery on the site and today this abbey church is St Alban's Cathedral. The site of Verulamium has been preserved as a park, and pilgrims still go there to honour England's first Christian martyr.

THINK ABOUT IT

It takes outstanding courage to stand by someone in need.

SAINT ALBAN
THIRD CENTURY

John the Baptist — First Century

Holy Days: 24 June, 29 August

All four Gospel writers tell us about John, who was a preacher and a prophet calling people to a change of heart (repentance). This was to prepare them for the coming of the Messiah. All the prophets of Israel had promised the people a future Messiah. They said, 'He is coming'. John was able to say, 'He is here.'

Luke tells us that John was the son of Elizabeth and Zechariah, and a cousin of Jesus. As a young man he went into the desert to become a hermit, a man of prayer. He probably lived in a community of religious people called the Essenes. He thought deeply about God and lived a strict life. Then he left the desert to preach on the banks of the River Jordan. He was a fierce and enthusiastic preacher, demanding that everyone should come to be baptised in the Jordan to prepare for the coming Messiah.

The Jordan was important to the Jewish people because it was at this river that they had first entered their promised land of Palestine. This was after their great 'exodus' from the desert, in the days of Moses. People flocked to hear John and many became his disciples. One day Jesus joined the crowds by the river and presented himself for baptism. John recognised that Jesus was the Messiah and said, 'I ought to be baptised by you.' But Jesus chose to be baptised by John, seeing his going into the water and rising out of it again as a preview of his death and resurrection. Later on John pointed Jesus out to some fishermen by the Sea of Galilee, saying, 'Look, this is the Lamb of God.' They immediately followed Jesus.

The Gospel writers point out how the life of John, the last of the prophets, was like a bridge between the Jewish expectations of a future Messiah and the New Testament coming of the Messiah – Jesus. John is important because he was the first witness and immediate forerunner of Jesus. He is like the athlete who carries the flame and runs into the olympic stadium to announce the olympic games. Even in his death he was a 'forerunner', by proclaiming the sort of fate that awaited Jesus; for John was imprisoned and put to death too. But this was not before Jesus had recognised the great holiness of his cousin. He said, 'I assure you that John the Baptist is greater than any man who has ever lived.'

Think about it

Prophets suffer because people don't like to hear the truth.

SAINT JOHN THE BAPTIST

PETER — FIRST CENTURY

HOLY DAY: 29 JUNE

His name wasn't always Peter. His parents called him Simon. He had a brother called Andrew and they lived by the Sea of Galilee and grew up to become fishermen. Not far away Jesus had grown up in a carpenter's family. Perhaps Jesus did some work on the boats down by the seashore. One thing is certain, he noticed Simon and was impressed. When Jesus wanted others to help him preach about the Kingdom of God, he was quick to ask Simon and Andrew to leave their nets and follow him.

Simon was strong and enthusiastic. He was always the first to jump in and offer his opinion. Unfortunately it was not always sensible; he used to speak first and think later. People called him a 'hot-head', but Jesus didn't mind this. He knew that Simon really meant to be supportive and enthusiastic about their work. So Jesus changed his name to Peter, which means 'a rock'. He knew that one day Peter would be brave and strong enough, like a firm rock, to be the foundation of the first Church communities. But it did not always seem like that.

The Gospel writer, Mark, tells a number of stories where Peter does not sound rock-like at all. He kept misunderstanding what Jesus told the group of twelve friends (we call them 'apostles'). We can imagine that Jesus sometimes shook his head in disappointment when Peter could not grasp what he was trying to tell him. But Peter never lost his enthusiasm, even jumping out of a boat to meet Jesus across the water. He eagerly promised his friend that he would follow him to the cross. But when it came to it Peter ran away, scared. He was devastated when Jesus died.

But an amazing thing happened. After the Resurrection a new Peter emerged. This time he was the 'rock'. He became the leader of the group of friends, and boldly led them to preach the Good News that Jesus had brought. The ordinary fisherman who sometimes messed up became the strong, determined leader of the early Church. He had a hard time setting up the new groups of Christians (followers of Jesus Christ). He travelled widely and finished up in Rome. There he was imprisoned and finally put to death, like Jesus, on a cross. He is buried in Rome and Catholics think of him as their first pope. That is why popes always live in Rome, in a place called the Vatican. Peter is good news for us all – saints aren't perfect people.

THINK ABOUT IT
A hot-head can become a dependable rock.

SAINT·PETER:

PAUL — FIRST CENTURY

HOLY DAY: 29 JUNE

I expect you know what a tornado is. It is a terrific storm that bursts over an area and it can cause massive destruction. There was once a man called Saul who was described as 'a tornado of enthusiasm and energy'. This Saul lived about the same time as Jesus, but never actually met him. Saul was a tent-maker and at that time people lived in tents out in the desert.

Saul was also a very enthusiastic Jew. After Jesus had died his friends began to preach that it wasn't the end of the story. Jesus was still alive, but in a new way. This upset Saul. He felt these followers of Jesus, now called Christians, were criticising his Jewish faith. So, like a tornado, he rushed through the country on a mission of destruction. He was going to kill all the Christians he could find.

But a very strange thing happened. He was riding to Damascus where he knew some Christians were preaching, when he fell off his prancing horse. He told his companions that Jesus had spoken to him. They didn't hear or see anything, but Saul was absolutely sure he had met Jesus. He changed completely and even changed his name to Paul – to prove he was a new man. He spent many years thinking about the way Jesus had lived and what he taught. Then Paul put all his energy into spreading the Good News about Jesus.

Over the next twelve years he made three enormous journeys. He travelled about 8,000 miles altogether. He stopped in towns and preached about Jesus, telling the crowds that they should become Christians. He set up groups of followers and wrote letters to them when he had moved on to other places. He called these communities of Christians his 'Churches'. His letters are full of kind messages and encouragement to ordinary people. But he was sometimes angry and got very annoyed with people who were being selfish and greedy.

Paul was the first missionary. Missionaries are Christians who go to other lands to spread the Good News about Jesus. Paul had many adventures and his life was very hard. He got into trouble with robbers, with the authorities, and his own Jewish people. He was imprisoned and even shipwrecked off Malta. Paul finished up a prisoner in Rome, where he was beheaded as a troublemaker. But Christians will never forget Paul, the 'tornado', who caused such an uproar that people had to sit up and listen.

THINK ABOUT IT

It is possible for people to change – even overnight.

SAINT·PAUL

BENEDICT B. 480

HOLY DAY: 11 JULY

The first people to introduce schools like yours into Europe were monks who followed the Rule of St Benedict. In fact much of Western history and culture have come under the influence of the monastic life. The example was set by a young Italian man called Benedict. He was born in Nursia, Italy, in 480. When he was 14 he was sent to study in Rome, but he wasn't very happy there. He hated the wild and immoral life of the Roman people of that time, so when he was about 18 he fled from the city into the deserted countryside.

Benedict joined some hermits in Subiaco and quickly became known for his holiness and wisdom. A few years later he was invited by the local hermits to become their leader. Over a number of years he founded twelve small communities of monks, including one on Monte Cassino. This became his final home. From there he wrote his 'Rule' for the life of prayer, study and work that the monks should follow. Although he asked for obedience to the Rule, he was a gentle and understanding father to the monks. He treated them as individuals and only asked what was possible and practical, although he couldn't stand grumblers. Benedict was loved and respected by everyone; although he was a determined leader he was never harsh. He radiated peace and calm, and humour.

When he was dying Benedict was taken to the chapel to receive communion for the last time. He died there, at the altar, and was buried in the same grave as his twin sister, Scholastica. She had lived a life of prayer just like her brother, and had died four years before him. Benedict had no idea how important his life would turn out to be. His Rule became the model for monastic life for centuries.

Today there are Roman Catholic and Anglican Benedictines across the world. Many live an enclosed community life within monasteries. Their lives are centred around daily Eucharist, sung community prayer and study. Benedict encouraged his monks to be self-sufficient: to farm the land, cook, write, keep bees, make wine or welcome guests to the monastery. And the monks have a long tradition of teaching; there are great abbey schools in England like Downside and Ampleforth, but your school can also thank St Benedict for making education important for everyone.

THINK ABOUT IT
Rules are important to make life run smoothly.

SAINT·BENEDICT

SWITHUN D. 862

HOLY DAY: 15 JULY

This saint's name is quite familiar in England, but we don't really know very much about him. There is a saying that if it rains on his Holy Day, which is 15 July, it will rain for the next forty days. No one seems to know why he became connected with the weather. There are similar stories told of three French saints. So here we have a mystery.

We don't know where or when Swithun was born; but we do know that he became a clerk attached to the West Saxon court of King Egbert. He was known for his learning and for his good life, so it was not surprising when the king chose him to be his personal adviser. Later he asked him to educate his son, Prince Ethelwulf. He must have done this well because Ethelwulf and then his son, Alfred the Great, ran a very honest and upright West Saxon court.

Swithun was made bishop of Winchester in 852. He was known to have developed the church buildings, but the present beautiful cathedral of Winchester was built two hundred years later, next to the site of Swithun's Saxon church. It is possible that Bishop Swithun was one of the first contributors to an important document called the *Anglo-Saxon Chronicle*. This is a history of England from the time of the Romans until the eleventh century. Started in the time of King Alfred, it was written by monks and recorded on a series of manuscripts.

When Swithun died he was buried in the churchyard, which is unusual for a bishop's burial. He had asked for this so that passers-by would walk over his grave and rain would fall on it. Is this a clue to the mystery of the weather tradition? Swithun's great reputation for holiness probably only began in Winchester many years after his death. When the Cathedral was built in the eleventh century, his bones were dug up and reburied in a shrine in the new building. It was a beautiful, jewelled monument and pilgrims from Europe always visited it on their way to St Thomas' shrine at Canterbury. One last mystery remains about St Swithun's story: When King Henry VIII stole all the jewels from churches and monasteries in 1538, he discovered that the gold and jewels on the saint's shrine were all fakes. How did that happen? Perhaps you could invent a good story about that!

THINK ABOUT IT

Can stories that are not true still be good stories?

SAINT SWITHUN

Grand Duchess Elizabeth b. 1864

Holy Day: 18 July

Have you heard of Queen Victoria? She was our Queen for 64 years. She married a German prince, Albert, and they had nine children. One of these married the German Duke of Hesse, but died when her daughter Elizabeth was only a child. Elizabeth was sent to England to be looked after by her grandmother, Queen Victoria.

Young Elizabeth was brought up in England as an Anglican, and attended church with her grandmother. When she was 20 years old she married a son of the Russian Tsar, with the name Grand Duke Sergei Alexandrovich. She chose to become a member of the Orthodox Church like her husband. The followers of Jesus have separated themselves into different groups, called denominations, although they remain united in following the teaching of Jesus.

As a member of the Tsar's family Elizabeth lived a comfortable life and grew strong in her faith. But she lived in uncomfortable times in Russia. There was a strong demand for a change in the way the country was governed. The Tsar and his government refused to respond. The people grew restless. In an uprising in 1905 Elizabeth's husband was killed. The event devastated Elizabeth and changed her life dramatically.

She gave away her jewellery and sold her precious possessions. She used the money to open the Martha and Mary Home in Moscow where she began to live a life of prayer and service to the poor. Over the years she was joined by many other women and they took the name 'Sisters of Love and Mercy'. They opened hospitals and looked after the poor in Moscow.

Only a few years later Russia was drawn into the Great War against Germany. The rule of the Tsar was over. Power was seized by a people's party, calling themselves Bolsheviks. They hated the Orthodox Church and began to imprison priests and nuns. Churches were destroyed. In May 1918, Elizabeth and two other sisters were arrested. The Tsar and his family were killed on 17 July 1918. Elizabeth and other members of the royal family were murdered a day later.

In spite of persecution Christianity has survived in Russia. Elizabeth continues to be remembered for her strength, faithfulness and kindness in the face of all opposition. In 1992 the Russian Church acclaimed her as a saint.

Think about it
Having riches doesn't always lead to happiness.

GRAND DUCHESS ELIZABETH
2001

Maximilian Kolbe b. 1894

Holy Day: 14 August

On 14 August 1941, Maximilian Kolbe, prisoner no. 16670, died in Auschwitz concentration camp after being injected with carbolic acid. His name was not always Maximilian. He was baptised Raymond, the second son of a poor Polish family. His father was a weaver. His parents were devout Catholics and taught the children to love Jesus and Mary before anything else. Honouring Mary was important to them, as she was someone who gave her whole life to God. Raymond, from an early age, wanted to be a martyr.

He went to the junior seminary in Lwow, and was top of the class in mathematics and science. Strangely, for a religious boy, he also became enthusiastic about the army and nearly gave up the idea of priesthood for a military career. But with his parents' encouragement he joined the Franciscans when he was 16 and took the name Maximilian. The brilliant young scholar was sent to study philosophy and theology in Rome. He was ordained priest there in 1918.

Maximilian never lost his enthusiasm for fighting, but he chose a new battleground by founding an 'army of crusaders' to fight for goodness. By becoming an expert in the media, Maximilian set out to spread his beliefs throughout Poland. He set up religious magazines and newspapers and was so successful that the Franciscans had to build an enormous monastery to house his work. Hundreds of young men joined his monastery until it had 762 members. But Maximilian wanted to be a missionary, so he went to Nagasaki in Japan. He taught at the university and did it so brilliantly that the Franciscans are still respected in Japan today.

Father Maximilian, now a sick man, returned to Poland as the war approached, assuring everyone that God understood their suffering. Germany invaded Poland and religious newspapers were banned. But Maximilian refused to stop publishing his newspaper, and was arrested and sent to Auschwitz. There he was beaten, kicked and lashed by the guards. But he spoke only of God's love to other prisoners, and shared his food ration with them. Everyone was amazed at his goodness, especially when he volunteered to take the place of a married man who was being sent to the punishment block. There he led hymns and prayers until his death. He achieved the martyrdom he had longed for as a child.

Think about it

How far would you go in helping your neighbour?

SAINT MAXIMILIAN KOLBE

Bernard b. 1090

Holy Day: 20 August

Do you like record-breakers? St Bernard was certainly one. When he became a monk he persuaded four of his brothers, an uncle, and twenty-seven friends to join the monastery with him! Bernard must have been a very popular young man. We are told he was handsome and intelligent, the son of a nobleman from Burgundy in France. He could have chosen to join a rich and powerful monastery where his family influence would have promised a comfortable career. But the enthusiastic group turned up at a struggling, local monastery that had recently been founded at Cîteaux.

The abbot was an Englishman from Dorset called Stephen Harding, who is also recognised as a saint. The monks at Cîteaux wanted to follow the Rule of St Benedict more rigidly than other Benedictine communities were doing, so it is surprising that Bernard and his friends went there. Even more surprisingly, they were followed by dozens more young men. Soon Abbot Stephen was able to send out groups of monks to start up similar communities across France. When it was Bernard's turn to leave Cîteaux he set up a monastery at Clairvaux.

It was a hard beginning. Bernard suffered from migraine headaches which did not help. But he learnt to be gentle towards others even when he was being hard on himself. He worked tirelessly and his influence spread so quickly that in no time he had founded sixty-eight new monasteries. Many people asked his advice, and he sometimes got into trouble for his strong opinions. Even bishops in Rome told him to stop speaking out. But he would not be quiet about some things: the privileged lives some priests were living and the persecution of the Jews. Bernard was also a great scholar and many of his books and sermons have remained popular even to this day.

The monasteries of St Stephen Harding and St Bernard are known as Cistercian foundations. The first one set up in England was at Rievaulx in Yorkshire. Its greatest abbot was St Aelred (born 1109) who was called 'the St Bernard of the north'. Six hundred men joined his monastery. Aelred made friends with everyone, including kings. He believed that friendship was a precious gift, and he asked his monks to see Jesus as a best friend.

Think about it
A good friend is more precious than gold.

SAINT AELRED
SAINT BERNARD

WILLIAM BOOTH B. 1829

HOLY DAY: 20 AUGUST

Do any of you play trumpets or trombones? A large group of Christians use brass bands in their worship and you sometimes see them marching to music through the streets. This is the Salvation Army. Less well known is their work of compassion. Members of the Salvation Army across the world feed the hungry, care for the sick and house the homeless. This work began with a Victorian gentleman called William Booth.

William was born into a poor Nottingham family. When he was only 15 years old, William became interested in Christianity and anxious to learn more about Jesus. He became a Methodist and before long worked as a preacher on Tyneside. He married a lady called Catherine and they had a large family. The couple were aware that Jesus had special concern for the poor and oppressed and were shocked that churches seemed to ignore the poorest people. They grew impatient and left the Methodist Church, moved to London and set up a Christian Mission in the poor East End. William's direct, honest talk and practical care appealed to ordinary people. He spoke out against injustice, especially condemning child labour and slavery. People began to listen seriously to him.

After some years, and feeling rejected by the Churches, William organised his work on a new, military model. He called his workers the 'Salvation Army'. He said he would fight to make people free. He wanted to save children from hunger, men from prison and families from sickness. And he did all this because this is what Jesus had done in his own day. William and Catherine put into practice exactly what they read in the gospels.

Today thousands of Salvation Army members, from New York to Australia, bring the Good News of the Gospel to alcoholics, single parents, prisoners and lonely people. They even search for missing persons and care for the homeless. The community members worship together, in prayer and music, as a way of gaining strength and encouragement for their difficult task. Their work goes on quietly, often unnoticed and usually unsung.

William and Catherine were an amazing and inspired couple. Catherine even became a preacher herself, one of the first women to take an equal place alongside men in the church. What is even more remarkable is that all members of the Salvation Army live on a basic wage, only sufficient for ordinary needs. They practise what they preach.

THINK ABOUT IT

Jesus said, 'Blessed are the poor.' Do we take this seriously?

WILLIAM BOOTH
B• 1829 D• 1912

Rose of Lima b. 1586

Holy Day: 23 August

St Rose is quite an unusual saint. Her real name was unusual to start with: it was Isabel de Flores y del Oliva, but she was always known as Rose. Her parents were Spanish but living in Lima, the capital city of Peru, in South America. Fifty years earlier, Spanish explorers led by Pizarro had taken the country from the Peruvian Indians. The Spanish treated the local inhabitants badly, taking their land and their most precious objects. By the time Rose was born, Lima was under Spanish rule and the local Indian people were being treated like slaves.

Rose's parents, Caspar and Maria, were hard working and serious about their religious faith. They were rather surprised, though, to discover that their young daughter was even more serious about it. They were worried because they thought she spent too long at her prayers and ate so little. When they fell on hard times Rose worked and worked to help them. She grew flowers to sell, and learnt to sew clothes and embroider tablecloths. She tried to do what her parents wanted, and loved to help them, but on one thing she would not agree with their wishes. They wanted her to get married but Rose said, 'No'.

She instead joined the third order of St Dominic. This meant that she could stay at home rather than join a convent of nuns, but she was attached to that religious order. Her family and friends were not happy because she was so strict with herself. She never joined in parties or went on holidays; she simply stayed at home, spending hours in prayer and penance (choosing to do things that were unpleasant). She even chose to live in the garden summerhouse on her own.

Everyone was surprised at her strange way of life; even the Church authorities came to question her about it. She said that she wanted to suffer because that is what Jesus had to do, and she wanted to be like him.

In the end people admired her strange holiness, because it made her very sympathetic to everyone who suffered, especially the Indians who had such a hard time from her own Spanish people. It is this that is remembered in Peru today and she is looked upon as the first real social worker in that country. The Indian population love her for standing alongside them when they were treated harshly.

Think about it

It is heroic to take on other people's suffering.

SAINT ROSE OF LIMA . . .

AIDAN OF LINDISFARNE

AIDAN OF LINDISFARNE D. 651

HOLY DAY: 31 AUGUST

You need to know some geography and history to understand this saint. When Christianity was first brought to Britain things didn't always go smoothly. Missionaries from Rome made Canterbury their headquarters, and Celtic missionaries from Ireland went to the north of England and Scotland. The two groups did things differently.

It began with St Columba who left Ireland to be 'a pilgrim for Christ' in the sixth century. He settled on the island of Iona on the west coast of Scotland and set up a flourishing monastery. Years later another Irish monk, Aidan, joined the community. King Oswald of Northumbria who knew Iona well invited monks from the island to preach the Gospel to his people. Aidan was consecrated a bishop and made his home on the island of Lindisfarne, on the east coast of England. From here he made journeys on foot far and wide and set up communities across northern England.

This caused some difficulty with the Christians based at Canterbury in the south, who also sent missionaries to northern England. The southern and northern Churches celebrated Easter at different times, and had some different rules. Bishop Aidan wouldn't change to fit in with the Roman bishops in the south. However, they admired and respected him so much that they agreed to disagree.

Bishop Aidan organised his monastery on Lindisfarne with great care. He was really happier being a monk than a bishop. He remained poor and would not let the community grow rich; he built only a small thatched church on the island, insisting that everything they had should be shared with the poor. He educated and trained English boys to become monks to help him in the missionary work. The north of England was soon converted to the Christian faith, through their work.

Everyone loved Aidan because he was kind and understanding. He was enthusiastic, but gentle in persuading people to accept the Good News about Jesus. The whole land grieved when he died in 651. He was buried on Lindisfarne and many Christians today still visit his beloved island.

THINK ABOUT IT
It is possible to agree to disagree.

SAINT AIDAN
OF LINDISFARNE

GREGORY THE GREAT b. 540

HOLY DAY: 3 SEPTEMBER

There have been sixteen popes called Gregory. Pope Gregory I is the best known and the most important. He is certainly important to the English, because it was he who sent missionaries to England to teach the people about Jesus. He was a brilliant leader of the Church.

Gregory was born in Rome, the son of a wealthy senator, and grew up during a bad time for the Roman Empire. It was at war. He became the chief magistrate in Rome and could have looked forward to a bright legal and political career. But Gregory was a prayerful man, and the chaos around him made him think again. When he inherited his father's estates he turned them into seven monasteries, including the family mansion in Rome. He called it St. Andrew's and chose to live there as a simple monk.

Four years later the pope sent him to Constantinople as his ambassador. He took some monks with him, so that he could continue the prayerful community life. After seven years he returned to his beloved St Andrew's Abbey in Rome, this time as abbot. But when the pope died three years later Gregory was asked to succeed him. He was a perfect choice because both the Roman state and the Church were in so much disorder. It needed a holy man to put things right and Gregory was that man.

As pope, he became organiser, politician, judge, social worker, writer, preacher, and reformer. But at heart he remained an ordinary monk. As the empire fell apart, it was Pope Gregory who took on the protection of Rome. It was devastated by the plague at this time, so he had to feed the people too. He changed the way land and buildings belonged to the Church, and made enough money to help the victims of the war and the plague. He reformed the way people worshipped, and took great care to train priests and bishops.

Gregory had always wanted to convert the pagan Saxons, and he found the way to do it. It is said he saw some fair-haired Anglo-Saxons in Rome and said, 'They are not Angles, but angels.' He immediately sent a group of his monks from St Andrew's to England. They were led by one of his monks who later became St Augustine of Canterbury. Today the Archbishop of Canterbury leads the Church of England. Gregory was pope for fourteen years and is admired as a great leader, statesman and doctor of the Church. He preferred to call himself 'the servant of the servants of God'.

THINK ABOUT IT

Being in charge means looking after people.

SAINT · GREGORY · THE · GREAT

Mother Teresa b. 1910

Holy Day: 5 September

A very small, elderly nun died a few years ago and the whole world seemed to mourn. Perhaps you can remember seeing her on television – a bent figure with a wrinkled but kind face? She wore a white cotton sari, edged in blue. This was Mother Teresa, a Catholic nun who worked tirelessly to protect the most lonely and vulnerable of outcasts.

Mother Teresa was born in Skopje, Albania, in 1910. Mr and Mrs Bojaschiu were grocers and called their daughter Agnes. She was quite a thoughtful and serious little girl. When she heard about life in India through the missionary priests who wrote to her parish, she decided that she must go out there to work with the poor. She was only 17 when she left her home and country to become a Loreto missionary nun in Dublin. She made her religious vows as 'Sister Teresa' and went to India to teach at St Mary's High School in Calcutta.

Sister Teresa always encouraged her pupils to help the poor. But after many years as a geography teacher she felt she had to do something more. She was embarrassed by the contrast between the comfort of the convent and the uncomfortable lives lived by the beggars and the dying in the street. She asked permission to leave the Loreto nuns in order to work with the poor. She rented a room in the slums; took a course in basic nursing and nursed the sick on the streets. She was soon joined by some of her former pupils, and in 1950 she and twelve of them became the first sisters of a new Congregation, the 'Missionaries of Charity'.

The authorities gave Mother Teresa a disused building where she took the dying off the streets. The Congregation grew quickly as hundreds of educated young women chose to live a strict life of great poverty. The sisters only possess two sets of clothes, a pair of sandals and a crucifix. They sleep in dormitories, eat simply and travel by foot. They spend several hours in prayer before they go to work with the sick, the dying, abandoned babies, orphans, lepers and poor families.

Mother Teresa became known world-wide. She spoke to world leaders; received awards for her work; was praised by the Pope and other Church leaders; but above all, was loved by the thousands of poor people whom she helped. She founded the Missionary Brothers of Charity to work alongside her sisters; and a number of other organisations.

Mother Teresa has not offically been called 'a saint', but her extraordinary love for outcasts makes her very special.

Think about it

'Let us do something beautiful for God.'

Mother Teresa

CALCUTTA
MOTHER TERESA
B• 1910 • D• 1997

Vincent de Paul b. 1580

Holy Day: 27 September

Many years ago there lived a very ambitious and adventurous young Frenchman, called Vincent. His parents had a farm and Vincent spent hours each day looking after the sheep. There were six children and not much money, but young Vincent was bright and keen to become a priest. His father had to sell some of the farmland to pay for his studies.

As a young priest Vincent was determined to live comfortably. He was furious when cheated of some money that had been left to him and crossed land and sea in search of the thief. On the high seas he was captured by pirates, and even sold as a slave. He escaped and met an Italian priest who took him to Rome and gave him a job in the court of King Henry in Paris. There he could have led a comfortable life, but the queen, Margaret of Valois, changed everything. She took him to visit the hospitals in Paris and he was shocked by what he saw. The sick and dying were huddled together on filthy straw.

Vincent changed. He suddenly saw two 'worlds' side by side. One was rich, powerful and selfish. Even some priests were lazy and uncaring. Rich families fought each other and religious people argued. The other 'world' was poor and powerless. Children had no schools and people were often hungry and sick. Vincent found a way to change this. He got his rich friends to help the poor. He told them that they were all God's children. He reminded them that Jesus helped everyone, rich and poor.

Many of the wealthy ladies whom Vincent had met in the palace offered to help. He was a very good organiser and soon there were groups of helpers in schools, hospitals and in the homes of the poor. One lady, a widow, was so keen to help that she left her elegant house and founded a community called the Daughters of Charity. Today she is known as St Louise de Marillac. Before she died her nuns were running orphanages, schools and hospitals across France, and even in other countries. The nuns today also work in homes for the aged and in hostels for the homeless.

Vincent formed an organisation of priests to preach the Gospel and work for those in need. When Vincent was an old man he wrote letters to encourage them. Over 4,000 letters are read today by his followers, the Vincentian Fathers. His wonderful work still goes on.

Think about it

Comfort others before you comfort yourself.

SAINT-
VINCENT-
DE-PAUL

Francis of Assisi b. 1181

Holy Day: 4 October

Francis was always happy. He had a loving mother, home comforts, good looks and many friends. His father, Signor Bernardone, was a wealthy cloth merchant. They lived in Assisi, a small hillside town in Italy. Francis led a carefree life, and as a young man spent most of his time with his friends, meeting girls or riding his horse.

During his lifetime there was fighting in Italy. Francis was an adventurous knight, and in 1201 he eagerly took part in an attack on nearby Perugia. But his side lost and he was held prisoner for a year. Then he became quite ill. He had time to think about his life. One day he walked to a ruined church, San Damiano. There he seemed to hear Jesus speak from the cross: 'Francis, rebuild my falling church.' He was so keen to start that he sold some of his father's cloth to buy the bricks. His father was furious and he threw him out.

Francis stripped off his rich clothes, put on a rough tunic, and left. He was penniless with nowhere to live. He knew it would be hard, but Jesus had said: 'If anyone wants to come with me, he must take up his cross every day, and follow me.' Everyone was amazed to see how happy Francis was, and some of his friends followed him. They walked all round Italy telling the people about God. They even went to Rome and the Pope gave them his blessing. They lived in huts and had no possessions. They accepted any kind of work in return for food.

Francis and his friends were so happy that many others joined them. And this included Clare, a friend from Assisi. She left home secretly and went to a convent to learn how to be a nun. She was joined by many young women who chose to live like Francis in complete poverty. They stayed in their convent praying and working quietly, praising God for his goodness. Francis travelled far, even trying to be a missionary among Moslems. Everyone, even the animals, loved Francis. People said that a fierce wolf sat down gently at his feet. He talked to the birds, telling them how much God cared for them. He wrote songs, praising God for the beautiful world he created.

Francis was 45 when he died. His followers are called Franciscans. There are many Franciscan priests, nuns and brothers today.

Think about it

We don't need to be rich to be happy.

SAINT CLARE
OF ASSISI
SAINT...
FRANCIS
OF ASSISI

Teresa of Avila b. 1515

Holy Day: 15 October

There are two saints called Teresa, both of them Carmelite nuns. The Carmelite Order began in the thirteenth century, when the English hermit Simon Stock wrote a rule for monks and nuns whilst he was living on Mount Carmel in Israel. His Carmelite monasteries spread across Europe. Three centuries later, a young Spanish woman joined one of them in Avila. She was called Teresa de Cepeday Ahumada.

Teresa was a lively and gifted young lady, and surprised her parents when she left home. She loved her family and always remained home-sick for them. The young nun surprised the community too, because she was so determined to live a serious life of prayer. The Carmelite community in Avila weren't following Simon Stock's Rule very well. Teresa was to change all that. In time, and against much opposition, she reformed the Carmelite life. First she founded a new monastery where the Carmelite Rule would be kept strictly. This was followed by 18 other communities. Everyone found Teresa charming and good company, but she was also forceful and strong. She never took 'no' for an answer. She was practical and full of common sense, yet deeply prayerful. Her overwhelming love of God had a big influence on the whole Church.

Thérèse of Lisieux b. 1873

Holy Day: 1 October

Three hundred and fifty years after Teresa of Avila's death, a 15-year-old French girl followed her example. Her name was Thérèse and she was to die of TB only nine years later. It is most remarkable that only a few years after her death the Catholic Church officially proclaimed her a saint. We know about these two saints because both of them wrote about their lives. Teresa of Avila chose to write books about prayer, but Thérèse of Lisieux was asked to write her autobiography. It became a bestseller.

Thérèse described her 'little way' to God. Her life sounds simple, uncomplicated, and at times even dull, but she set out to do the most ordinary daily tasks in a spirit of love. She always smiled and never grumbled. No one guessed that she found this very difficult because she was in pain and often depressed. St Thérèse shows that very ordinary people can become very 'Christ-like'. But don't be fooled – it is more difficult than it looks!

Think about it

The saints did ordinary things extraordinarily well.

SAINT TERESA OF AVILA
SAINT THÉRÈSE OF LISIEUX

LUKE — FIRST CENTURY

HOLY DAY: 18 OCTOBER

When St Paul travelled on his missionary journeys he sometimes took with him his friend, a doctor, called Luke. Luke was a Gentile (a non-Jew), and he soon became an enthusiastic disciple of Jesus. It is most unlikely that he ever met Jesus personally, but he learnt about him when he listened to Paul and other disciples speak about him.

Luke was so impressed by what he heard that he decided to write down, in an orderly way, all the stories that he heard about Jesus. Luke was a scholar and could write in a good Greek style. The two books he wrote make delightful reading, and tell us much about Jesus and the first years of the Church. His two books are the Gospel of Luke and the Acts of the Apostles.

Mark, Matthew and John also wrote Gospels, but none of them have the same warmth as Luke's. Luke emphasises the compassion that Jesus showed towards the poor, the outcasts and people whose lives were in a mess. Perhaps, being a doctor, Luke could identify with the day-to-day sufferings of ordinary people. He also noted the complete ease with which Jesus dealt with women, treating them as equals – something unheard of in the culture of the time. Luke liked the way Jesus accepted everyone as equal. He alone has kept a record of the story told by Jesus in which the hero is a Samaritan, whom Jews of that time despised.

Luke was impressed by the effect that Jesus had on all those who heard him, and accepted him as the Son of God bringing God's Kingdom into the world. His Gospel is full of examples of the stories Jesus told to make people sit up and think. The message repeated many times by both Jesus and Luke was that the Kingdom of God is for everyone. Luke had a great dream which he saw Jesus beginning to fulfil, that love could break down all barriers of race and culture.

The angel's message to the shepherds in the opening pages sums up Luke's whole Gospel: 'I am here with good news for you, which will bring great joy to all the people.' Luke was a happy, contented person; no wonder Paul wanted him as a travel companion on his long journeys.

THINK ABOUT IT
Making everyone welcome brings much joy.

SAINT·
LUKE:
1ST·CENTURY·

Martin de Porres b. 1579
Holy Day: 3 November

To be a child of mixed-race parents can be difficult. It shouldn't be though, because every person is loved by God. Martin lived in Peru in the sixteenth century. He was a 'mulatto', that is, his father was a white Spaniard and his mother was an Indian from Panama. We don't know if he suffered from racial prejudice, but the United States have adopted him as patron saint of those who work for harmony and justice between people of different races.

When Martin was a youth he became a lay brother in the Dominican friary at Lima. A lay brother does not become a priest, nor can he become a leader of the community. Instead he serves the priests, and takes all the most humble jobs in the house and garden. Martin spent all his life serving others this way. He was the community barber and infirmarian (the one who looks after the sick) and he spent many years as a farmer, growing food and caring for the animals.

It is said that Martin was so kind and good that he could never turn anyone away from the friary gate. The beggars crowded outside waiting for their friend to give them food and comfort. He showed great concern for all the farm animals, and would not even hurt the smallest fly or the insects that attacked his plants. It is hardly surprising that people outside the friary began to hear about this kindhearted and approachable lay brother. Normally they would have turned for help to the priests, who were educated thinkers, teachers and leaders.

There are many stories about Brother Martin showing brilliant judgement in advising his own family and other families. He sorted out marriage problems, raised money for his niece's dowry and even became the adviser to local government officials. It isn't surprising that stories grew up about him doing quite impossible things. But there is no doubting his holiness. When he died everyone in Lima called him a saint. It seems strange that the Church only acknowledged this a few years ago. In the 1960s when there was much racial hatred in the news, the Catholic Church chose at last to honour Martin with the title of Saint. He is a reminder that God created all people equal, whatever their race, colour or education.

Think about it
Enjoy people's differences. It makes the world exciting.

SAINT MARTIN DE PORRES

Frances Cabrini b. 1850

Holy Day: 13 November

Francesca Maria was the youngest of thirteen children of an Italian farming family. Even as a child Francesca was very strong-willed and determined that one day she would become a missionary in China. Although she was often unwell, she worked very hard at school and later became a teacher. Then she applied to become a nun, but two convents refused her because of poor health. Instead the bishop asked Francesca to take charge of an orphanage.

It was not easy at the orphanage but the bishop noticed how hard Francesca worked. He called her one day and said: 'I know you want to be a missionary. I don't have a missionary Order of Sisters. Found one yourself.' And she did, with six young women who had been in the orphanage. They were called Missionary Sisters of the Sacred Heart. They struggled with little money and suffered considerable opposition from a senior bishop in Rome. But her communities grew, and this meant a delighted Francesca could now go to China, a dream that she had never lost. In 1887 Mother Cabrini, as she was now called, was in Rome. The Pope told her that she must go, 'not to the east but to the west'.

The Pope was concerned for the thousands of poor, illiterate Italians who had emigrated to the United States. They were being treated badly and exploited by agencies who only wanted to make money. The Italian government refused to help, and local Americans hated them. They ended up desperate and crowded together in 'little Italies' across America. The Church came to their rescue. A bishop founded the Society of St Charles in New York to care for immigrants, and Mother Cabrini offered her services. This transformed the Italian communities. Her sisters, against unbelievable opposition and disasters, won the hearts of the American people. They set up schools, hospitals and charitable organisations across America, welcoming not only Italians, but anyone in need.

The work later spread across the world. Mother Cabrini's faith, business sense and strong will amazed her critics. She never took no for an answer. American Catholics are proud that she chose to become an American citizen. And today America is proud of Italian-Americans who are prominent in politics, sport, business, education and medicine.

Think about it

Refugees and immigrants must be treated with dignity.

SAINT FRANCES CABRINI

Margaret of Scotland

Holy Day: 16 November — b. 1045

It is remarkable how many British kings and queens are honoured as saints. Quite a number of them lived at a time when England was conquered by different races. Margaret of Scotland is one of these saints. She was born in 1045, when her English father, Prince Edward, was living in exile at the court of the king of Hungary. The family moved back to England when Margaret was 12, and lived at the court of another saint, King Edward the Confessor.

The Normans came from France and conquered the English in 1066. So Margaret's family were on the move again, this time to Scotland. The Scottish King Malcolm soon fell in love with the gentle Margaret, and asked her to marry him. She hesitated because she had intended to be a nun, but finally agreed. It was a wonderful marriage. Malcolm was not too well educated, but through Margaret's influence he became a good and wise leader. He was known as Malcolm Canmore which meant 'The Great Ruler'. He followed his wife's example and became full of compassion for the sick and the poor, and he grew to love the Church.

Margaret was a wonderful mother to their six sons and two daughters. She also spent much of her time looking after orphaned children and the poor. She made beautiful vestments and altar cloths for the church. Margaret was a great queen who was able to solve problems without causing conflict. She encouraged the Celtic Catholics in Scotland to sort out problems with the English Catholics who were guided by Rome. Scotland had been cut off from the rest of Europe, and with remarkable skill Margaret introduced the best European culture (way of life) into her country.

It is said that Queen Margaret and her sons brought a 'golden age' to Scotland. This lasted for two hundred years after her death, when her sons continued to rule with the same honesty and compassion. Sadly, there was some unrest in Scotland towards the end of her life. Her beloved husband was killed by a rebel army near Alnwick; Margaret died only four days later in Edinburgh Castle. They were buried at Dunfermline Abbey which they had founded together. Their son David, who became king, is also honoured as a saint in Scotland.

Think about it

It is the busiest people who have time for others.

SAINT MARGARET OF SCOTLAND

Elizabeth of Hungary b. 1207

Holy Day: 17 November

Imagine a princess who lived long ago, in a far-away land. Do you think of turreted castles, beautiful dresses, banquets, servants and handsome princes? Well, not all princesses are like those in the story-books. St Elizabeth certainly wasn't. She was a princess though, daughter of the king of Hungary. And when she was only 14 she did marry a prince, Louis of Thuringia. And they did live in a castle, Wartburg castle in Germany.

The young couple were very happy, although life was not always comfortable for them. Louis was a very good king and husband, but his mother was unkind and jealous of Elizabeth. She was no help when Elizabeth had her three children, and constantly made fun of her daughter-in-law. This was because Elizabeth didn't want to be a rich queen, living in beautiful surroundings, eating rich food and wearing expensive jewels. Instead, she wore simple clothes and gave money and gifts to the poor.

Elizabeth helped her husband govern his kingdom, but she was happiest looking after their children, visiting the sick and the poor, and spending time at prayer. Her mother-in-law thought that this was no way for a queen to behave. After only six years of marriage, King Louis died when he joined the crusader knights who went to win back Jerusalem from the Moslems. Elizabeth was heartbroken. To make matters worse, the royal family threw her out of the castle and made Louis' brother king. She had nowhere to go, and spent the first few days among the farm animals, trying to keep her children warm.

Fortunately, Elizabeth's uncle was a bishop. When he heard what had happened he rescued her. She found someone to care for the children and devoted the rest of her short life to looking after the poor. She asked a priest to guide her so that she could try and live a holy life; but he was quite cruel and made her life very hard, demanding that she send all her friends away. Elizabeth never complained and quietly made new friends with the poorest people. She made clothes for them, and even went fishing in order to feed them. Everyone grew to love her. She was only 24 when she died, tired out by loving other people more than she loved herself.

Think about it

Giving to the poor is better than trying to be rich.

SAINT
ELIZABETH
OF HUNGARY

HILDA — B. 614

HOLY DAY: 17 NOVEMBER

When Hilda was 13, no one could have imagined how important she was going to become. She would have been very surprised herself. Hilda grew up in Northumbria and was a relative of King Edwin. When he was baptised by Bishop Paulinus of York, the whole family followed his example. Twenty years later Hilda decided to become a nun.

Bishop Aidan of Lindisfarne heard about the intelligent and devout nun, and shortly before he died he made her abbess of a convent at Hartlepool. After a few years she founded a new monastery on the cliff-top at Whitby. It was a double monastery, where monks lived in one building and nuns lived next door. Hilda was the abbess in charge of the whole community and was a very successful and strong leader. At this time there was a quarrel going on between Christians in the south who followed Roman traditions, and Christians in the north who followed Celtic ones. A conference was called to settle the argument, and the bishops chose Whitby as their meeting place. Under Abbess Hilda's guidance the discussions went smoothly, and although she personally supported the Celtic Church, it was decided that everyone should follow the traditions of Rome and the Church of Canterbury.

Many people travelled to Whitby to be advised by Hilda: kings, princes, and bishops, and ordinary people also. They had heard of her holiness and wisdom and knew she would welcome them. It was said that all who knew her called her Mother, such was her gracious godliness. She was very concerned that her monks and nuns should do some serious study of Scripture, and she insisted that priests should be properly trained for their task.

In fact, Hilda believed that everyone should be encouraged to develop their talents. She invited one of her herdsmen, Caedmon, to become a monk so that he could make use of his love for writing verse. He became the first English poet. Another of her monks became Bishop of Hexham and later Bishop of York. He is honoured today as St John of Beverley. By the time Abbess Hilda died in 680, she was loved and respected throughout the land.

THINK ABOUT IT
Don't hide your talents. Use them.

quoniam
SAINT HILDA

CECILIA B.?

HOLY DAY: 22 NOVEMBER

Do you play a musical instrument? If not, you probably still like music of some kind, and have your favourite pop star or group. There is a saint who is specially remembered for her love of music She is St Cecilia of Rome. The story of this martyred saint is not at all clear; in fact, very little is known about her. The story that grew up about her, and was written down about the year 500, is not based on much historical evidence.

This is how the story goes: A noble Roman family had a daughter who wanted to live a life of prayer. Her parents thought differently and found her a husband. They arranged her marriage to a young man called Valerian. He was not a Christian and was surprised when Cecilia told him that she did not want to live with him as his wife. She said that as the music was playing during the ceremony, 'she sang in her heart to Christ'. (This is her connection with music.) She persuaded Valerian and his brother Tiburtius to become Christians. For this, they were at once condemned to death. It was very dangerous to be a Christian.

Cecilia was arrested too, and taken back to her own house to be smothered in the steam of her own sauna. This failed, so a soldier tried to behead her. This failed too since she took three days to die from the wounds. Her last act was to ask for her house to be turned into a church. This is only a story, but it was built around some known historical figures.

There is evidence that in the third century a lady from the Cecilii family in Rome gave her property to the Church. This included land which became the cemetery of Pope Callistus. The Cecilii family relatives were buried there. The lady also gave a house to the pope, and he turned this into a church. It is also known that there were two martyrs called Valerian and Tiburtius, though they had no connection with the lady.

The story of St Cecilia is the result of early Christians wanting to praise the enthusiasm and courage of those who were martyred for believing in Jesus. They said that the faith of those first Christians is something worth singing about. Cecilia may not have been a martyr, but she was generous and loved the Church. So Christians still sing her praises.

THINK ABOUT IT
What do you do that is worth singing about?

SAINT CECILIA

ANDREW — FIRST CENTURY

HOLY DAY: 30 NOVEMBER

Have you ever made a discovery or got interested in something new, then along comes your brother or sister and takes over? You might feel annoyed, or leave them to it and go off to find another new interest instead. This could have happened to the brothers, Peter and Andrew. They were fishermen from Bethsaida, and they had a house by the Sea of Galilee at Capernaum.

Andrew had been a disciple of John the Baptist. One day John pointed Jesus out to him, saying, 'This is the Lamb of God.' Andrew hurried to his brother, Peter, and took him along to Jesus, who later told them both to leave their fishing nets and follow him. Jesus also invited their fishermen friends, the brothers James and John, to join the group. These were the first four of the team of twelve helpers whom Jesus chose, and we know as the twelve Apostles. From the very beginning it was Peter who became the leader of the twelve. His brother Andrew remained more quietly in his shadow. Peter, James and John are often mentioned in the Gospels as being very close to Jesus. Andrew is missing from the special group. We have no idea how he felt about it. There is a hint in the Gospels that he might have made friends with Philip. Anyway, he didn't go off in a huff because his brother had stolen the limelight!

We know quite a bit about Peter, but very little about Andrew. That does not mean he was unimportant. If he had not listened carefully to John the Baptist he may never have discovered Jesus, nor taken Peter along to meet him. Christians have always honoured him for being the very first disciple of Jesus. It is thought he went to Scythia and Epirus and then to Greece. He was martyred there, at Patras, for being a follower of Jesus. There is a tradition that he was bound to an X-shaped cross, where he remained for several days preaching to crowds before he died.

Andrew is the patron saint of Scotland. There is a legend that the man who guarded his relics at Patras was told in a dream to take a relic of the saint to a place God would show him. He was led to Scotland and built a church at the place we now call St Andrews. Scotland's flag, proudly waved at international football and rugby matches, is the blue cross of St Andrew. The quiet saint is not forgotten.

THINK ABOUT IT

Quiet, trusted team members are as important as the leader.

SAINT
ANDREW
1st CENTURY

NICHOLAS — FOURTH CENTURY

HOLY DAY: 6 DECEMBER

You ought to know all about St Nicholas because he is the patron saint of children. He became so popular in the eleventh century that he was also made patron saint of countries (especially Russia), dioceses, cities, churches, sailors, merchants and pawnbrokers. This suggests he was a very important person indeed. But all we actually know about him is that he was a bishop of Myra in Lycia, south-west Asia Minor, in the fourth century. And we know that in 1087 some Italian merchants stole the relics, believed to be those of Nicholas, from Myra, and built a shrine for them in Bari, Italy. The Italians loved this saint, and pilgrims flocked to the shrine. He soon became known as St Nicholas of Bari.

He was certainly loved very much by the early Christians because so many legends grew up around him. A legend is a story that may not be accurate but it tells a truth about the person. The legends about Bishop Nicholas tell us that he must have been a generous, kind man, who always wanted to help people in trouble. He was a humble man too, because he didn't want to be thanked for his generosity; he helped people secretly and never wanted a fuss made of him.

The most famous legend is the story of three sisters whom Nicholas is said to have saved from poverty when he heard that their father could not pay for their marriages. The bishop threw three bags of gold coins into their window at night. Other stories were told of Nicholas saving three men from death when they had been unjustly accused of crimes. He is also said to have rescued sailors in distress.

In Holland, Germany and Switzerland children receive presents from Saint Nicholas on 6 December and they eat gingerbread men. Here in England and in America he has become known as Santa Claus, a name which comes from a Dutch dialect for 'Saint Nicholas' – Sinte Klaas. It is a pity that today most people in Britain only think of him as the cuddly, white-bearded Father Christmas figure, who carries a sack of toys and rides with the reindeer. It might be a very good idea to turn Father Christmas back into Saint Nicholas, as a reminder that Christmas is a Christian feast day. You could start by designing a card of Saint Nicholas for 6 December.

THINK ABOUT IT
When you help someone, do it secretly.

SAINT NICHOLAS

STEPHEN — FIRST CENTURY

HOLY DAY: 26 DECEMBER

Martyrs are those people who suffer and die for their beliefs. Across the centuries, thousands of men and women have died rather than deny their religious beliefs. The first Christian martyr was Stephen. His story is told in chapters 6 and 7 of the Acts of the Apostles, written by Luke.

In the very early days of the Church, the apostles chose seven deacons to assist them in their work. Luke says that the first of these seven was Stephen, 'a man full of God's grace and power'. Stephen was probably a Greek-speaking Jew, because he was asked to look after the Greek-speaking widows in Jerusalem's Christian community. He was also an enthusiastic preacher, very anxious to share the Good News proclaimed by Jesus.

His preaching angered other Greek-speaking Jews, especially a group known as the Congregation of Free Slaves. They did not like his enthusiasm for Jesus, so they bribed people to accuse him of speaking against Moses and God. The authorities were notified, and Stephen was called before the Jewish Religious Council, called the Sanhedrin. He stood before the Council and gave a long explanation of his faith in Jesus. He did this by outlining the history of the Jewish people. He concluded, 'Your history shows you have never listened to God's Word. You have always resisted the Holy Spirit, and now you have betrayed and murdered the Holy One.'

Stephen's words infuriated the Council. They had him dragged from the city and stoned to death. Following the example of Jesus to the end, Stephen forgave the men who were killing him. Luke describes the scene: 'While they were stoning him, Stephen prayed, "Lord Jesus, receive my spirit." Then he fell on his knees and cried out, "Lord, do not hold this sin against them." When he had said this, he fell asleep.' (Acts 7:59-60)

Stephen was chosen to assist the Apostles, which he did with absolute faithfulness and enthusiasm. He is a fine example for all those who work behind the scenes.

THINK ABOUT IT

Could a court find evidence to convict you of being Christian?

STEPHEN
FIRST CENTURY A.D